Yorkshire Dales
A to Z

by W. R. MITCHELL

DALESMAN BOOKS
1974

35p.

THE DALESMAN PUBLISHING COMPANY LTD.,
CLAPHAM (via Lancaster), NORTH YORKSHIRE

First Published 1972

Second Edition 1974

© W. R. Mitchell, 1972, 1974

ISBN : O 85206 266 4

An Introduction

The A to Z of the title should not be taken to imply that every worth-while fact about the Yorkshire Dales is included in this booklet. Space considerations alone decree that it should have far less pretentious aims.

Here, in alphabetical order — with X as a notable omission — is a selection of Dales subjects in which an alert, non-specialist visitor to the Dales National Park might be interested.

Each subject is covered by brief, factual information. The booklet may therefore be taken as a potentially informative companion in the Dales or as a work supplementary to other Dales publications. I hope that it will at least be entertaining.

W. R. M.

Printed in Gt. Britain by GEO. TODD & SON, Whitehaven.

Front Cover Illustration of Hubberholme by Alec. Wright. Section Illustrations by Stanley Bond.

A

Abbeys: After the Conquest, monastic orders received gifts of land from the great lords (Scrope, Clifford, Percy) and many lesser landowners. Most prominent in the Dales were the Cistercians, who originated at Citeaux in France. Partly because they refused to benefit from the manorial system and were enjoined to work for all their income, the Cistercians settled in remote places; they exploited the wilderness, specialising in sheep. Cistercians established Jervaulx (the name a French version of Yoredale, now Wensleydale), and it was active from 1147 until 1537. The most extensive monastic rights in the Dales were, however, exercised by Cistercian abbeys standing outside the area — by Fountains (near Ripon), Furness (near what is now Barrow-in-Furness), Sawley (between Gisburn and Clitheroe), Rievaulx and Byland (near Helmsley). The highly successful pastoralist monks had outlying farms called *granges,* manned by layfolk, but also reared cattle and horses and mined lead. The profits from their various enterprises were invariably used in ambitious building programmes. (See BOLTON, COVERHAM, EASBY, FOUNTAINS, JERVAULX, also PRIORIES).

Addlebrough: Table-topped hill (1,564 ft.) near Bainbridge, Wensleydale. Name derived from Old Norse, Authulf's Burgh. Romans who established a fort at Bainbridge are reputed to have had a summer camp on Addlebrough.

Agriculture : (See FARMING).

Aire, river : Source at Aire Head Springs, below Malham. The river, which crosses the axis of the Pennine uplift by way of the Aire Gap, has a total length of 65½ miles, of which 15½ miles are tidal. A stream emerging from the base af Malham Cove is popularly supposed to be the Aire but is derived from water sinking at Haw Knabs, near the chimney of the old smelt mill on Malham Moor. Known as Malham Beck, this water courses under a clapper bridge near the Cove and also under the equally quaint Moon Bridge, which is believed to have taken its name from a Prior at Bolton, Wharfedale.

Ais Gill : Ais Gill beck, a tributary of the river Eden, is located on the former border country (the North Riding and Westmorland). The beck is spanned by a railway viaduct (87 yards long) on the summit stretch of the Settle-Carlisle line (1,169 ft. above sea level).

Angles : A Germanic people who entered the dale country from the east, mainly in the 7th century, and settled primarily in the valleys, in which they did much land reclamation by drainage and timber clearance. Danes were other settlers, also seeking valley sites. Anglian placenames are frequently suffixed by *ley* (clearing in a wood) and *tun* (farmstead with its surrounding wall). An example of the former is Wensley; Grassington typifies the latter. Danish placenames frequently end in *by* and *thorp*.

Angling : Highest branch of the sport in the Dales is fly-fishing for brown trout. Dark beck trout, running to four or five in the pound, must be approached with skill and cunning. Grayling, a species that usually stays close to river bottoms, occur in Ure, Wharfe, Swale, Ribble and Aire. Pike are found in the middle and lower reaches of some rivers. Bream in Semerwater. (See CRAYFISH, FISH, SALMON).

4

Apedale : Small valley near Castle Bolton, Wensleydale. It was not the haunt of apes but a possession of a Norse settler called Api.

Architecture : Initially caves provided shelter. In later times circular stone huts, thatched with ling or turf, were commonly used. Cruck-building was a feature for centuries before building with stone and slate. The first substantial stone buildings, castles and large churches, date from 12th and 13th centuries. Skills developed by masons were employed by Dales yeomen following the dissolution of the monasteries and the consequent changes in the ownership

Richmond Castle and the Swale
(drawn by Alec E. F. Wright)

5

of the land. There was a boom in stone building in the latter part of the 17th century, following the unrest of the Civil War and increasing prosperity of the farmers. Many of the unpretentious but attractive upper Dales farmhouses date from this period. (See BARN, BYRE, CRUCK-BUILDING, DOORHEADS, FARMHOUSES).

Arkengarthdale : Also known as Arkendale, this is a tributary valley of the Swale, branching off n.w. from Reeth and extending towards Tan Hill. Name means "the valley of Archil's enclosure." The Lords of Ravensworth owned the Forest of Arkendale. This district was also notable for lead-mining, reminders of which are still to be seen. There are the remains of a powder house not far from the *C.B. Inn,* which was named after Charles Bathurst, a prominent mineowner. (See BOOZE, WHAW).

Art : The Dales country, with its transient weather, usually calls for swift action by an artist : it is thus pre-eminently water-colour country. The late Marmaduke Miller, of Arncliffe, considered that March and April were the best months for water-colour painting, explaining : "Then you have very little green; the dominant colour is a warm, dull, yellow ochre."

Aysgarth Falls : Aysgarth, in Wensleydale, has a name derived from Eik Skard, "open space with oaks." At the lower waterfalls the river Ure tumbles over bands of the Yoredale series of rock. There are three groups of falls. Near the upper falls stands a large mill and a single-arch bridge with a span of over 70 feet.

Azilians : Early visitors to the Dales area, arriving about 8,000 years ago in small groups to hunt and fish. They are named after caves at Mas D'Azil in France where their remains have been particularly well preserved. A limestone cave near Settle yielded a reversed barbed harpoon of reindeer antler believed to be of the Azilian period. The harpoon is preserved in the Pig Yard Club at Settle.

B

Bain, river: Reputedly England's shortest river, $2\frac{1}{2}$ miles long, cutting a way mainly through glacial debris from Semerwater by Bainbridge to the Ure.

Barden Tower: Ruined hunting lodge between Bolton Abbey and Burnsall, in Wharfedale. The lodge stood in the Forest of Barden. It was virtually rebuilt by Henry, 10th Lord Clifford (1485-1524), and restored by Lady Anne Clifford in 1658-9.

Barguest: A spectral hound. (See TROLLERS GILL).

Barn: Name is from Old English *bere-aern,* or *bern,* meaning "barley house." In the Dales it is the farm outbuilding in which hay is stored and some cattle are wintered. There are good examples of *tithe barns* at Bolton Abbey and Lawkland. Where a barn and farmhouse occupy a single capacious roof the term is *cote* or *coit.* The most imposing barns are in Craven, being large, with double doors, often with a substantial porch. The actual cowshed is known in Craven as a *shippon.* Features common to many Dales barns are: *mow, mew* or *mewstead,* usually pronounced "moo" (storage space for bulk of hay); *threshingstead* (stone-flagged area where threshing took place and now carts with hay are drawn in for off-loading); *balks* (timbering over the stalls, used for part of the hay crop); *boose* (standing place for stock); *boskin* (partition between groups of booses); *fothergang* (passage). (See BYRE, LATHE).

7

Bartle, burning of : Custom of burning an effigy, "Owd Bartle," at West Witton, in Wensleydale, on St. Bartholomew's Day, August 24. Effigy is previously borne down village street and traditional verse recited.

Beamsley Hospital : Almshouses established in 1593 by Margaret, mother of Lady Anne Clifford, and added to by Lady Anne, 1650-60. Buildings stand beside the A.59 not far from Bolton Bridge, Wharfedale. Quaint circular chapel with a diameter of 30 feet.

Bees, bee-keeping : Some walled gardens have recesses, *bee boles,* in which straw skeps containing bees were placed. Stocks of bees had to be destroyed before the honey could be collected. An American, Rev. L. L. Langstrath (whose family is believed to have originated in upper Wharfedale) observed that bees leave a space of 5/16" between their combs. This discovery led to design of hives with hanging frames which can be moved at the discretion of the bee-keeper.

Besom : Used for sweeping rough ground, such as cobblestones. Dales besoms were invariably made of ling, with a staff of ash or elm. The ling was bound to the head of the shaft with ash saplings.

Birds : Some typical nesting birds — golden plover and dunlin (high, broken ground), red grouse (moorland), meadow pipit and skylark (mostly rough grassland), short-eared owl (rough grassland, new plantations with abundance of voles), kestrel (cliff faces), snipe and redshank (marshy areas), black-headed gull (beside moorland tarns), curlew (fell edges, and increasingly in the valleys), lapwing (marginal land, meadows and pastures), raven (few pairs on high crags), wheatear (scree areas, walls), great-crested grebe (larger lakes and reservoirs), sandpiper (lakes and rivers), oystercatcher (rivers with shingle beds), dipper and grey wagtail (streams), yellow wagtail (waterside meadows), carrion crow (isolated trees), jackdaw (cliff faces, some church towers), swallow and house martin (farmhouses and buildings).

8

Right : Almshouses at Beamsley

Stanley Bond.

Birds, vernacular names: *Laverock* (skylark), *blackoozle* (blackbird), *water ousel* (dipper), *dunnock* (hedge sparrow), *ruddock* (robin), *moorgame* (red grouse), *hullet* (owl), *chucker* (fieldfare).

Bishopdale : Tributary valley of Wensleydale, extending from near West Burton to Kidstones Pass (1,400 feet), beyond which lies Wharfedale.

Bolton Castle : Fortified house in Wensleydale built by Richard Scrope, the construction work beginning (according to Leland) in 1379. Mary Queen of Scots was kept prisoner here (1568-1569). Within the castle is a folk museum.

Booze : A corruption of *bowehous,* which is Old English for "house by the bow or curve." Name for a cluster of farms in Arkengarthdale, off Swaledale.

Boulder Clay : Deposit left on the melting of a glacier, consisting of scoured material. (See ICE AGE).

9

Bridges : Some early bridges erected to facilitate transport between properties owned by monasteries. "Devil's Bridges" (such as Dibble near Hebden, Kilgram near Jervaulx) may have been built with attendant human sacrifice, to placate the river spirits. Most graceful bridges are possibly the single-span structures associated with packhorse traffic, examples of which are Thorns Gill (North Ribblesdale), Ivelet (upper Swaledale). (See CLAPPER BRIDGE).

Brigantes : Hill folk who came into prominence at the time of the Romans, being a federation of Iron Age tribes that resisted them. A possible reason for Roman expansion into North was subjugation of these people, following the breaking of a treaty. A Brigantean patriot, Venutius, had a 170-acre stronghold at Stanwix, near Barnard Castle. Here the Brigantean cause was defeated in 74 A.D. Some of Brigantean prisoners were set to work in the lead mines, an occupation with which some of them would already be familiar. It is believed that the Brigantes made the fortification wall at the summit of Ingleborough.

Buckhaw Brow : The stretch of A.65 climbing to the watershed to the west of Settle; where the road dips beyond is known as Cave Ha'. Traffic moves roughly on the line of a geological fault, which was responsible for the fine scars of Giggleswick. Notice that both limestone and gritstone are represented in the walls at the point where the fault occurs.

Buttertubs : The name of a pass rising to 1,726 feet between Wensleydale and Swaledale. Named after limestone shafts, each about 60 feet deep, lying beside the pass and supposedly shaped like old-fashioned tubs.

Byre, Cow : A type of small farm outbuilding seen at its best in Swaledale. Contains loft for hay storage and tying-up for four beasts. Such buildings, handy to the meadows, enabled the quick transportation of hay to storage undercover in "chancy" weather.

C

Canoeing : Has never been a popular sport, partly because of objections by anglers. The main dales rivers are canoeable as follows : Ribble from below Settle; Swale from Grinton Bridge; Ure from Askrigg. Over 70 miles of the Wharfe is negotiable, with portages at turbulent stretches such as the Strid.

Castles : They stand at strategic points round about what is now the National Park. Several in the Eden Valley (Appleby, Brough, Pendragon) guarded northern approach by Scottish marauders. Skipton Castle was built with oversight of the Aire Gap. Richmond Castle is on a cliff above the Swale and Barnard Castle with a similar dominant site by the Tees. Wensleydale, which is broad and fertile, has two castles, Middleham and Bolton. The latter is more of a fortified manor, occupying a position less capable of being defended than a true castle.

Cattle : Craven was noted for long-horned breed. This was succeeded by the Shorthorn, the Dales variety being the Northern Dairy Shorthorn which is red-and-white, small and hardy. The brown-and-white Ayrshire, with upswinging horns, was also kept in dairying areas and was noted for producing abundant milk after grazing poor pastures. The dominant breed today is the black-and-white Friesian, descended from importations from the Low Countries and noted for its lean meat and outstanding milk yield. On the hills, black-and-white animals are reared as dairy replace-

11

ments or for beef, but here there are also beef herds in which the Galloway and Aberdeen Angus strains are prominent. The most recent immigrant is a docile, grey, beef breed of French origin, the Charolais.

Cattle Terms : They vary with different areas. In Craven, an animal is a calf at birth — either a heifer (female) or a bull (male). Between the ages of 10 months and 12 months it becomes a stirk (known as a steer elsewhere), either a heifer or a bull stirk. Bull stirks not suitable for breeding are castrated and become bullocks for beef production. An animal aged 18 months is a heifer or a bull. Heifers are put to the bull usually at the age of 2 years; they then have two broad teeth testifying to their age. Two additional teeth are acquired in the following year. At the age of four, the animal has a "full mouth."

Cautley Spout : A waterfall tumbling from the Howgill Fells and seen clearly from the Sedbergh-Kirkby Stephen road. The grand amphitheatre in which the waterfall is set is partly of glacial origin. There is a footpath to the Spout from near the *Cross Keys* (National Trust).

Caves and Potholes : Limestone is dissolved by rainwater which has collected carbon dioxide in the atmosphere and vegetation. The erosion has produced complex underground systems, about 1,000 of which are known on the Yorkshire Pennines and adjacent areas. Potholes ("pot" being a Norse word for a deep hole) are vertical shafts where the streams gain entry; caves are the points of egress, above the impervious older rock. Of the potholes, Gaping Gill (Ingleborough) has a main shaft which is 340 feet deep, measuring from its floor to the bed of the entering stream. The total depth of Gingling Hole (Fountains Fell) is over 590 feet. Three cave systems open to the public are White Scar (near Ingleton), Ingleborough Cave (near Clapham) and Stump Cross Cave (Greenhow, between Grassington and Pateley Bridge).

Cave Fish : Usually lacking pigment and the ability to see. Such albino fish have been reported from several underground systems, including Great Douk Cave (Ingleborough). The fish recovered here were about eight inches long, of a dullish-white tone, with faintly discernible spots. Lid-like growths had formed over the eyes, which were smaller than the eyes of normal trout.

Cave Formations : Calcium carbonate dissolved by rainwater is held in solution, to be redeposited through evaporation in the form of mineral calcite. The resulting cave formations include : *stalactite* (hanging from a cave roof), *stalagmite* (growing upwards from a cave floor) and *curtain* (extending from roof to floor, usually at the side of a cave passage). Salts taken from minerals through which water has passed give distinctive colours : green (copper ore), white (limestone), red (ironstone), grey (lead). (See LIMESTONE COUNTRY).

Cave Remains : Remains of ancient animal life and objects used by Early Man have been preserved in caves. Excavation at caves near Settle revealed deposits laid down in a warm interglacial period, when the local fauna included lion, hippopotamus, rhinoceros, hyena, sabre-toothed tiger, elephant. In more recent deposits were remains of Ice Age creatures, including woolly rhinoceros and the great cave bear. Later still, relating to immediate post glacial times, was evidence of reindeer, Arctic fox, hare, bison, brown bear and wolf.

Chapel-le-Dale : A valley extending from near Ingleton to Ribblehead, with Whernside to the north, Ingleborough to the south. The chapel, now St. Leonard's Church, is served from Ingleton. Within it is a plaque commemorating the men who died during the construction of the Settle-Carlisle railway. Over 200 people from the shanty towns at Ribblehead were interred in an enlarged churchyard (1869-1875).

Cheese : Cheese was originally a useful means by which more primitive man, who lived precariously, could "lock up" the protein of milk produced in spring and summer for consumption at a later time. In the late 13th century, ewe milk was being used for cheeses on monastic estates. Such cheese was sent from Malham Moor to Bolton Priory, from Fountains Fell to Fountains Abbey, and from the holdings of Jervaulx to the main Abbey. Milk from the Shorthorn cow was later used by farming families through whom the cheese-making tradition continued. Factory methods were introduced in late Victorian times. The best-known Dales cheeses were Wensleydale, Swaledale, Cotherstone (Teesdale). They were actually made to the same formula in roughly the same circumstances.

Cheese, Wensleydale : Wensleydale is a soft cheese. There are noticeable differences between the modern factory product and that made by old methods on the farms. Farmstyle Wensleydale was mellow; it more or less melted in the mouth and had a nutty flavour derived from the high moisture content. Such cheese was eaten about eight weeks after manufacture and kept its quality for another 12 weeks. Modern cheese is made to be eaten in about a fortnight, and after 6 weeks it is becoming too old. Some farmhouse cheeses were being made up to the 1939-45 war. There is a Dales couplet that declares : "Apple pie without Wensleydale cheese is like a kiss without a squeeze."

Cheese, Whangby : Made out of either 100% skim milk, or half skim milk and half new milk. Because it did not contain the right percentage of butterfat it was hard, fit for nothing but cooking. The term was used as a symbol for toughness, viz., "tough as a whangby."

Cheesecake : A kind of tart, sometimes made in a saucer. The jam filling of a normal tart was replaced by a mixture of cheese-curds, eggs, sugar, butter and a little nutmeg.

Churches : Crosses were raised where itinerant preachers addressed the people. First Dales churches were of Anglican origin, and buildings of special antiquity are frequently marked by prefix *Kirkby* in the village name. Some Dales churches with special features are : *Swaledale* — St. Agatha, Easby (13th century frescoes, terra-cotta and black); St. Andrew, Grinton (Norman font). *Wensleydale* — St. Michael the Archangel, Spennithorne (Norman arches, 13th century screen); Holy Trinity, Wensley (Flemish brass, Bolton family pew). *Wharfedale* — St. Michael and All Angels, Hubberholme (rood, loft, pews by Thompson of Kilburn); Priory Church of Bolton (walls of monastic origin, enclosing the former priory nave); St. Wilfred, Burnsall (early Norman font, pieces of Anglo-Danish gravestones). *Malhamdale* — Kirkby Malham (perpendicular style, 14th century oak chest). *Ribblesdale* — St. Oswald, Horton (Norman font, stained glass showing mitred head of Thomas a Becket); St. Alkelda, Giggleswick (Norman work, 17th century woodwork, stained glass based on theme of ebbing and flowing well and featuring the probably fictitious patron, Alkelda); St. Mary, Long Preston (Hammerton tomb, Jacobean pulpit).

Clapper Bridge : Consists of large slabs of stone on simple piers. The word is from medieval Latin, *Claperius,* meaning "head of stones." Two clapper bridges near Austwick have been spoilt by renovation work in modern idiom, rails and concrete. There is a clapper bridge close to a single-span packhorse bridge at Linton (Wharfedale).

Climate : Cold, dry conditions followed the retreat of ice. Warmer conditions from about 6,000 B.C., with the spread of broadleaved trees over former tundral areas. Bronze Age man (c.3,000 B.C.) enjoyed warm, dry conditions, encouraging the colonisation of former untenable areas. Wet and cold weather had returned by about 500 B.C., which was the period of rapid peat formation in upland areas. Since Bronze Age there have been fluctuations between continental types of climate and maritime conditions. (See WEATHER).

Climbing: Dales speciality is limestone climbing using artificial aids. Two outstanding climbs are in Gordale gorge (Malhamdale) and at Kilnsey Crag (Wharfedale). The latter, with its enormous overhang, is climbed only with special permission from the owner.

Clint: Name given to surfaces of bare rock on limestone pavements. A fissure between clints is known as a *grike,* and some of these, greatly eroded, developed into potholes. *Grikes,* which are frequently deep, shady and damp, can support a rich and varied plant life, especially ferns.

Clocks, Clock-making: Case clocks of late 17th, 18th and 19th centuries are still moderately common. John Ogden, of Bowbrigg near Askrigg (Wensleydale) was making such clocks in the 1680s. He and his apprentices gave Askrigg renown for fine clock-making. Men trained at Askrigg set up successfully elsewhere. Decline of Dales clock-making was partly attributable to the inflow of cheaper Yankee clocks.

Clough, river: Rises (as Grisedale Beck) on Baugh Fell, becoming the Clough in Garsdale and flowing westwards to join the Rawthey, which in turn is a tributary of the Lune.

Coal: Was mined in the Dales from at least the 13th century until the transport revolution which enabled coal to be brought into the area by rail. In the early days coal was needed for lime-burning and mining as well as for domestic use. Dales coal was taken from thin seams high on the fells, including Fountains Fell and Tan Hill. Small pits were in use between Dentdale and Garsdale. The old track serving them has now been given a hard surface, but is still known as the Coal Road. In Wensleydale, the Metcalfes worked

Turner Fell pit, a *day hole* supplying coal to the greater part of the valley; the enterprise closed about 1910.

Colt Park : Twenty-one acre ash wood on long limestone scar, the best example of its type in the country. It occurs on the lower slopes of the north-east face of Ingleborough, four miles n.w. of Horton-in-Ribblesdale. Administration is by the Nature Conservancy, Merlewood, Grange-over-Sands.

Corpse Way : Ancient track from head of Swaledale to Grinton, later named Corpse Way because it was used by funeral parties travelling to the parish church at Grinton. Bodies were borne in wicker baskets. The route lay on the north side of the valley, over Kisdon to Muker and thence by Iveletside. Its use by funeral parties was discontinued on the consecration of church and graveyard at Muker.

Cotterdale : At the head of Wensleydale, entered by way of five-barred gate. The King family were once the best-known farmers in Cotterdale. This valley has been planted with conifers.

Cotton Grass Bogs : Known as "mosses," an example being Foul Moss at the top end of Kingsdale. Mosses are extensive on high ground which has considerable rainfall, usually land over 1,250 feet. Appearance is normally a pale green from sphagnum moss, but is enlivened in summer by the white downy seed heads of cotton grass (*Eriophorum vaginatum*), another of the great peat-forming plants of the Pennines.

Coverdale : Bleak 12-mile tributary valley of the Ure. Leland wrote that it was "worse than Swaledale or Uredale for corn and hath no woods but about Coverham Abbey." This abbey (established 1212) has long been ruined. Miles Coverdale, translater of the Bible into English, is believed to have been a native of the valley.

Cowhouse : Also known as mistal and shippon, local variants. (See BARN, BYRE).

Cranesbill : Blue meadow cranesbill (*Geranium fratense*) is abundant in many parts of the Dales. The name *fratense* alludes to meadows; in fact, this plant has been found growing tenaciously up to 1,000 feet above sea level. Charles Kingsley, the writer, admired cranesbill in "the high hills of Craven."

Craven : Name for a wapentake, also an archdeaconry, occupying the western part of the National Park, including the limestone country and a part of Bowland. Being starker than areas to the east, the name is said to be derived from "land of crags." Also suggested is a Welsh origin from *craf*, a reference to garlic!

Crayfish : The scientific name for the freshwater crayfish is *Astacus*. The creature is found in most rivers, frequenting the deeper, stonier stretches, and also occurs in Malham Tarn and Semerwater. Camden noted that Sir Christopher Metcalfe (1513-1574) introduced crayfish to the Ure. Here they have been specially protected, an angling bye-law stipulating that "the cray fishing season shall begin on August 10 and end on September 30." Only the claws and flappers contain edible flesh. The claws are cracked open by hammer.

Crooks : (See SHEPHERDS' STICKS).

Crow, carrion : Common corvine, generally detested by sheep farmers and gamekeepers because of its predation on weakly lambs and the eggs and young of game birds. Known as *crake* in Swaledale, where a local placename, Crackpot, is said to be derived from "the hole where crows abound." Has also been called *ket-crow*, from a name for offal. A crow has a uniformly black plumage and is feathered at the base of the powerful beak.

Cruck-building : Early form of building involving *crucks* or *forks*, which are curved trees sawn down the middle, reared on the ground and united at their apices by a *ridge tree*, the

18

general effect, when thatched, being of a boat turned upside down. Originally, the feet of the crooks were set on stone to keep them above the ground; later they were placed on walls to make more space available within the structure.

Crummackdale : Valley between Long Scar (Ingleborough) and Moughton Fell, approached from Austwick. (See ERRATICS).

Curlew : Largest of the European waders, streaky-brown plumage, long legs, decurved bill. Curlews spread widely over the Dales to nest and winter at the coast. Dales birds usually move south-westwards, some to the tidelines of Eire. The bubbling call of a cock curlew in its territory is among the most appealing of Dales bird calls.

Cycling : Cycling clubs centred on the industrial towns are frequently seen in the Dales. Some cyclists, preferring the "rough stuff," follow green tracks across the fells formerly used by monastic traffic and packhorse trains. Each autumn, cyclists storm the Three Peaks — Ingleborough, Whernside and Penyghent — in a race that begins and ends at Horton. The 25-mile course, involving 5,000 feet of climbing, is regarded as the most gruelling cyclo-cross in the world and has been completed in less than 3 hours.

Feizor, in the limestone country (drawn by Charles Hurford)

19

D

Dale : From the Old Norse *dalr,* meaning valley. Drainage made the first cuts into an ancient plateau, and these water-eroded valleys were generally of V-shape. The conspicuous U-shape is a testimony to the abrasive character of the ice sheets that moved across this area, overtopping all but the highest summits. Glaciers broadened, deepened and polished the old valleys, coating parts of the sides with *boulder clay.* Most recent deposits in the dales are *river alluvium.*

Dalesmen : Men of the western fell areas are said to have characteristics of the old Norse colonists. They have been realistic, conservative, independent, taciturn, thrifty — yet capable of great hospitality. In the valleys, Anglo-Danish characteristics are detectable.

Dales Way : Riverside walk, based mainly on the banks of Wharfe and Dee, between Ilkley Bridge and Bowness-on-Windermere. First announced in 1968, and first traversed in 1969 by Venture Scouts from Bradford, who took $3\frac{1}{2}$ days over the journey. It could become an official long-distance footpath.

Dee, river : Flows in Dentdale, its main feeder developing on Blea Moor. The river's upper reaches are noted for the beauty of water-eroded limestone.

Deer : In the tundral conditions after the retreat of the ice, there was summertime grazing on lichen, browsing on dwarf willow, by reindeer which wintered in the forests. Skeletons of reindeer have been found in Stump Cross Cave (Green-how Hill). Red deer were well represented in the Dales fauna, first in the wild, when they were celebrated beasts of the chase, then in parks, which represented — apart from sporting considerations — a handy "protein bank" to be drawn on in winter. Most of the parks were clear of deer by the end of the 18th century. Today there is a small herd of red deer, owned by a farmer, on Long Preston Moor (Ribblesdale). Roe deer are present in some of the lower dales and have also appeared in a newly-afforestated area at the headwaters of the Wharfe. (See FORESTS).

Dent "marble": Not a true marble, being one of several varieties of dark, fine-textured limestone, rich in light grey or white fossils, once used enthusiastically for fireplace surrounds. The "marble" trade of the upper valley of the Dee developed during the 18th and was at its peak in the 19th century. It went into rapid decline when a tariff was lifted on the importation of Italian marble about 1890. In Arten Gill, power for marble-quarrying was provided by an iron waterwheel 60 feet in diameter.

Dialect: Generally speaking, from the point of view of speech, Wharfedale forms a natural boundary and splits the dale country into two. To the north, the speech is softer, less aggressive than in the West Riding section. This is evidenced by the northern utterance "thoo gurt feeal," compared with the West Riding "tha gre't fooil." Many words and turns of speech date back to the Anglo-Danish colonisation; many more words were added by the Norse settlers who came in from the west.

Dipper: Known in some parts of the dales as *water ouzel* and in others as *Bessie Dooker,* this is a small bird of fast-flowing streams. It appears uniformly black in colour but is really a very dark brown with a white "bib." It exploits an unusual food niche, the beds of streams, collecting such morsels as caddis larvae. Its domed mossy nest is usually found beside a waterfall or under a bridge.

Dogs: (See SHEEPDOGS).

Doorheads: A striking feature of much Dales architecture, especially in the Settle area. Dates on doorheads range mainly from 1640 to 1740. The ornamentation usually includes the initials of the owner plus, occasionally, a sundial.

Drovers: An increase in the demand for meat by an increasing urban population in England led to an extension of the old droving trade with Scotland, Wales and Ireland. The Scottish trade affected the Dales most, for several important routes passed through the district; fairs were held and Scotch cattle grazed before re-sale in the markets of the Midlands and South. The drovers were not just "bullock-wallopers." Some were wealthy enough to employ drivers to move the herds. Craven graziers visited the Highlands to purchase stock. One of them, a Mr. Birtwhistle of Skipton, could offer 5,000 Scots cattle at a time at sales held on the Great Close, Malham Moor.

E

Early Settlement: Man has been present in the Dales area for about 10,000 years. At first small tribal groups lived by hunting and fishing, using the drier limestone areas and avoiding, where possible, the dense woodland and swampy ground. Limestone caves were used as sanctuary. From 9,000 to 6,000 years ago hunters of the Mesolithic (Middle Stone Age) were active. The folk of the Neolithic, or New Stone Age, period (from about 5,500 years ago), developed a more settled, pastoral life. It was at this time that man burst out of his natural niche and began his progress towards dominance of his environment. There was expansion in the Bronze Age, which is marked in the Dales by the erection of stone cairns and burial mounds. The Dales have a number of native rural settlements of the Iron Age and Roman period. Some of the best are in the Grassington district (Wharfedale).

Earthquakes : Generally of a minor character, occurring when there is a strain on the boundaries of a geological fault and pressure is suddenly relieved. The last important Pennine tremor was in 1970. The basic cause of Pennine shudders are faults in the Askrigg Block. (See FAULTS).

Easby Abbey : About a mile from Richmond, in Swaledale. Founded by Premonstratensians in 1155.

Emigration : Drift from the land is an old problem. Some people were forced out by the emparkment of land and improvement in farming methods. Enclosures of common land that began towards the end of the 18th century, and industrial depression — both farming and mining — in the 19th century, were later major causes of depopulation.

Enclosures : (See FIELDS).

Erratics : Rocks moved by glacial action to areas where they would not normally occur. A classic area is Norber Fell, near Austwick, where a glacier moving down Ribblesdale and Crummackdale broke off pieces of Silurian rock and deposited them on the limestone of Norber. Such rocks, being impervious to water, remained and protected the limestone immediately beneath them from the weather. These rocks were eventually standing on limestone pedestals.

F

Farming : For many years small, updale units that ceased to be viable were merged to form larger units. Today, on some of the old farming land, large-scale afforestation with conifers has taken place. Farming life in the upper dales is mainly concerned with stock-rearing, both cattle and sheep. Customarily, ageing sheep are drafted from the hills for cross-breeding to produce Mashams. Suckler cattle are kept for beef production. Lower down the dales, much dairy farming takes place, with several important recent changes. Silage-making as opposed to haymaking is becoming more common. There is loose-housing of stock instead of the tying up of individual cattle in a byre or shippon. Milking parlours have generally replaced the laborious task of milking with units, which in turn succeeded hand-milking. (See CATTLE, SHEEP).

Farmhouses : In remoter areas, the type of building is comparatively little changed from that of early Norse and Danish settlers, who had permanent *winter houses* and temporary summer homes (*saetrs*), where people remained near their stock at the hill grazings. Early types of wooden and rough stone construction, thatched with ling or sods, gave way to farmhouses of local stone. The movement began in the 16th century and continued with a veritable building boom in the 17th century. Main features of the 17th century farmhouse; flagged roof, the pitch depending on the weight of slate used; mullioned windows (an imported Tudor style); projecting stone porch; carved and often dated doorhead. (See DOORHEADS).

24

Faults : Dislocations in the rocks of the earth's crust. In parts of the Dales there has been a displacement of several thousand feet. The main faults in the National Park are the Craven and Dent Faults. The former is split into three major systems — north, mid and south. A fault line can be spectacular because of the abrupt changes of landscape. For instance, the Great Scar Limestone, covering a large area to the north of the mid-Craven fault, disappears quickly from sight to the south of the faults. The transition between limestone and gritstone is clearly seen at Giggleswick Scars and in the Malham area.

Fell : Old Norse name (*fell* in Iceland, *fjell* in Norway) for high hills. Striking examples are the Three Peaks — Whernside, Ingleborough and Penyghent — which are isolated. They rise from a limestone plateau as residual fragments of the strata of an ancient plateau. Some of the highest fells in the Dales National Park are : Whernside (2,414 feet), Ingleborough (2,373), Great Shunner Fell (2,340), Great Whernside (2,310), Buckden Pike (2,302), Penyghent (2,273), Hugh Seat (2,257), Great Coum (2,250).

Fell-Walking : Generally an informal pastime, but the Boy Scouts organise two annual hikes — the Fellsman (for seniors) and Dalesman (for juniors). Both take place in the Craven Dales. Each spring a Three Peaks Race is held; it evolved from a walk over the summits of Ingleborough, Whernside and Penyghent. The Pennine Way is the longest continuous footpath in Britain. (See PENNINE WAY).

Fields : Historically, a name for cleared woodland. Some fields are of great antiquity. Bronze Age folk had fields and stock enclosures. The arable fields of Romano-British times are clear to see above Grassington. The three-field system did not always work in the classical way partly because of inclement weather and an old preoccupation with stock-rearing. Population pressures in the 12th and 13th centuries led to land being *assarted,* or taken in from the waste. At some medieval enclosures, known as *vaccaries,* cattle were ranched. Land enclosed by a lord of the manor (*park*) enabled an improvement in farming techniques by regularisation. The great period of enclosure occurred in the 18th and 19th centuries (generally from about 1750 until 1850), when the rectangular fields (*allotments*) were created. Many straight though not necessarily level stretches of roads date from period of enclosure. The Commissioners tended to work from a map using pencil and ruler.

Fish : (See ANGLING, CRAYFISH, SALMON).

Fleet Moss : Crossed by the motorist between Oughtershaw and Gayle, the road being the highest stretch in the National Park (1,934 feet). Fleet Moss was much earlier crossed by a Roman road extending from the fort at Bainbridge towards the head of Ribblesdale.

Floods : Regular flooding in the Ribble valley below Settle, with the most serious floods occurring at roughly 10-year intervals. Some serious occasional floods are noted. During one flood at Upper Wharfedale (June, 1686) 100 acres of land was washed away and a further 100 acres in the Kettlewell district covered with stone and gravel. Kettlewelldale was flooded up to 15 feet deep in 1881. A writer about Dentdale in 1891 described the view at floodtime as "like looking over Grasmere." Over 5 inches of rain had fallen in 30 hours!

Flowers : The flora is at its most varied on the limestone. Here there is an adequate rainfall and maximum drainage. Some distinctive limestone area plants are yellow rock rose, dwarf yellow viola, bird's eye primrose, globe flower, water avens, marsh marigold. In boggy places can be seen the Grass of Parnassus and the butterwort. There is a much more limited flora in peaty areas because of the lack of oxygen in the peat. A plant associated with lead refuse, and thus found in a few selective areas, is the spring sandwort.

Flowers, Arctic : Some plants that colonised the upper dales immediately after the retreat of the ice survived in isolated colonies because of a fortunate combination of geology and climate. It is essentially a tundral flora, the conditions last obtaining generally from 12,000 to 10,000 years ago. Among the Arctic plants in the Dales is the purple saxifrage, flowering in March on inaccessible limestone cliffs, and the mountain avens. The best-known flower community of this type is on *sugar limestone* at Cow Green, Teesdale, part of which has now become a reservoir. The plants here include spring gentian, Teesdale violet and bog sandwort.

Forests, Forestry : Native species of trees that are still prominent include ash, hawthorn, yew and hazel. The term *forest,* of Norman origin, was related to land set apart for game, invariably for the sporting use of the king. Dales forests were mainly at the daleheads, on the poorest land. Attendants lived in *lodges.* Among the Dales forests were : Wensleydale (valley above Bainbridge, south of the river), Bishopdale Chase, Arkengarthdale, New Forest (part of Forest of Stainmore), Swaledale Forest (above Reeth), Applegarth Forest (near Richmond), Barden Chase (Wharfedale). In the modern conifer forests, established on former grazing land, planting takes place mainly with sitka spruce. Hardwoods are planted in the gorges.

Fountains Abbey : Established in the valley of the Skell, near Ripon, and having considerable territorial rights in the Dales. Fountains Abbey, for instance, owned Malham West, and additionally received the gift of all Malham Moor and land extending over the fells to Littondale, including all the area now known as Fountains Fell. The old Norse sheep farms of Malham Moor were managed from a *grange* at Kilnsey.

G

Gaits and Stints : The definition of a *gait* varies from district to district, even from moor to moor. Generally, it is a term representing the pasturage of a single sheep with its followers from May 1 to the end of August. It might be arranged that 1 gait is the equivalent of 4 ducks; four gaits equal to 1 cow; 5 gaits to a horse. A *stint* applies if a moor is legally regulated, each farm having a claim to a specified number of gaits. The stint is said to be governed by the number of sheep that can be wintered on the in-bye land during the days when the moorland grazings are closed. It is based on the assumption that there is good quality heather on the moor, which may not now be the case because of overstocking with sheep. Originally, the system of gaits and stints was meant to avoid this circumstance.

Gaping Gill : Possibly the finest, and certainly the most spectacular pothole. Its deep main shaft is seen penetrating the east side of Ingleborough at a height of about 1,250 feet above sea level. A funnel-shaped depression leads to a sheer drop of 340 feet to the main chamber's floor. Miles of passages radiate from this chamber, and potholers seek to explore a link with Ingleborough Cave, one and a half miles away.

Garsdale : From Old Norse, meaning Garth's valley. Garsdale extends from near Sedbergh towards Wensleydale and is traversed by the A.684. Its river is the Clough.

Geology : Carboniferous rocks, laid down over a period of perhaps 75 million years, provide the dominant feature of the Dales National Park, excluding the Howgill Fells, which are more akin in formation to those of Cumbria. The carboniferous strata between Stainmore and the Aire Gap has been grouped under the term Askrigg Block, which rests on a core of granite, above which lie folded slates and grits. Some of these are exposed in the west, notably in the Ingleton district and in North Ribblesdale, the green and blue slates of Pre-Cambrian times being seen in the Ingleton glen below Thornton Force. Lying atop these folded rocks is Great Star Limestone (around 500 feet thick) that formed in a clear and shallow coral sea. Above the limestone are about 1,000 feet of the Yoredale Series, (a much-repeated sequence of harder and softer rocks, limestones, shales and sandstones laid down in fluctuating conditions). Finally, there is millstone grit, formed of a build-up of sediment in a delta. The Askrigg Block tilts gently towards the east. Consequently, there are great exposures of limestone in the west. North and east of the Park, the dominating feature is the Yoredale series, which gives a stepped appearance to the sides of valleys like Wensleydale. The millstone grit endures as remnants on the very summits of fells in the west and is extensive to the east. (See FAULTS, LIMESTONE COUNTRY).

Gold : C. J. Cutcliffe Hyne, who spent his latter days at Kettlewell, having as a youth travelled the world for material for his many books, went prospecting for gold and found minute quantities in streams above the village.

Gordale Scar : A limestone feature near Malham. Cliffs over 200 feet high overhang. Gordale beck descends through the gorge in a series of waterfalls over tufa-encrusted rock.

Grike : (See CLINT).

Gripping : Open moor draining, with trenches that are usually a foot wide and a foot deep. Care is needed to ensure that the *grips* are on the contours, otherwise rapid and unsightly erosion occurs.

Grisedale : Valley extending from Garsdale, named after old association with keeping of swine. Grisedale has been planted with conifer trees.

Grouse, red : A most distinctive Dales bird, being resident on moorland. The male was anciently known as "moorcock," a term perpetuated in the name of several inns, one being at the meeting point of roads from Wensleydale, Garsdale and Mallerstang. Whitaker, the historian, wrote that "hawking and netting for grouse was in use in the year 1725, when shooting flying birds was introduced to the great astonishment of the dalesman."

Hardraw Force : Name is also rendered Hardrow, being derived from *herde-raw,* or dwellings used by shepherds. The Force falls over a lip of rock and descends for almost 100 feet without disturbance. A careful visitor may walk behind the fall. Whitaker noted a great frost of 1739-40 when Hardraw Force became a hollow column of ice and "the unfrozen current was distinctly seen to precipitate itself through a tube in the centre." Blondin, walking the tight-rope over Hardraw, stopped in the middle of the rope to cook an omelette.

Haytime : Hay is grass that has been mown and left to dry in the fields, from which it is taken to the barns to be stored as winter fodder for the stock. Haymaking controls the annual rhythm of stock between high and low pastures. The animals are kept on higher land during the period when low-land grass is growing for hay. In the upper dales, haytime is late, the first flush of grass being consumed by the lambing ewes. Haytime here coincides with inclement weather in July and August! The grass growth following haytime mowing is called *fog*.

Haytime Labourers : Modern mechanisation has reduced the need for hired help. Previously, Irishmen were taken on for a month and, in 1900, the labour cost per man was about £4 a month. In hand-mowing a field several men worked as a team using scythes of enormous length. Refreshments taken outdoors between meals are known as *drinkings,* being referred to in Swaledale (1823) as *donfron.*

Heaf : From the Icelandic *hefta,* meaning to restrain, and known as *heagh* in the North Riding. A heaf is a tract of land, often without boundary walls, to which the native hill sheep become greatly attached. In some cases the heaf-going instinct (vital in areas where there are few if any boundary walls) is perpetuated by the landlord owning the flock. The tenant has its use and can benefit from wool and the sale of surplus animals.

Heather : (See MOORS).

Hell Gill : Deep ravine which until local government re-organisation in 1974 was on the Yorkshire-Westmorland border, between Wensleydale and Mallerstang. Contains an early reach of the river Eden, which then turns to flow northwards to Solway Firth.

Hornblower : Each day at 9 p.m., between Holyrood (September 28) and Shrovetide, a hornblower at Bainbridge (Wensleydale) sounds three blasts on the forest horn. On still nights the sound has been heard three miles away. The original horn is in the folk museum at Bolton Castle. That currently in use was presented to the village by Mr. R. H. Harburn in 1864.

Howgill Fells : The grassy hills (white bent mainly) dominating the Sedbergh district. The Howgills are composed of slaty rocks, of a more complex geological structure than geological systems to the east. The highest point at the Howgill range is the Calf (2,220 feet). The area is a traditional haunt of the Rough Fell breed of sheep.

I, J

Ice Age : During the Pleistocene, or Great Ice Age virtually all the Dales area was covered by ice and snow. Glaciers broadened and deepened the old river valleys and, on melting, left *drumlins* and expanses of *boulder clay*. When the ice had retreated, the area was first colonised by moss, lichen, grass, sedge, dwarf willow and birch.

Ingleborough : Highest point (2,373 feet) of a group of fells rising from Great Scar Limestone near Ingleton. Other fells in the conspicuous group include Little Ingleborough, Simon Fell and Park Fell. Ingleborough is capped by a 15-acre plateau on which the remains of an Iron Age hill fort have been found. The most popular approach to the summit is across Storrs Common, from Ingleton. A longer, more varied route takes in Clapham, Trow Gill, Gaping Gill and Little Ingleborough, thence along the skyline to Ingleborough's summit.

Jervaulx Abbey : A Cistercian house in Wensleydale, the nearest village being East Witton. The ruins are open to the public. The abbey was established in 1156 and dissolved in 1537. Jervaulx monks had a right to mine lead in the dale. They also reputedly made the first Wensleydale cheese, using milk from ewes.

K

Kilnsey Crag : In upper Wharfedale, dominating the village of Kilnsey, the Crag is given distinction by an immense overhang. Climbers succeeded in climbing the Crag by this route in 1957.

Kingsdale : Glaciated valley between Gragareth and Whernside, approached from Thornton-in-Lonsdale. The relatively straight road dates from the enclosures. A post-1939/45 war road now leads from its head to Dent. Yordas Cave, near the head of the valley, was frequently visited by the tourists of the Romantic Age.

Knitting, Hand : During the 17th and 18th centuries, hand-knitting was a major industry in small dales along the Yorkshire-Westmorland border. Vast numbers of stockings were despatched to Kendal market. Dent became the best-known centre for knitting partly because Robert Southey wrote a novel called *The Doctor* and coined the phrase "terrible knitters e' Dent." The word "terrible" in this sense means "great". Wool spun into a coarse thread of worsted for knitting was known in Dentdale as *bump*. The knitters of Dent were rarely seen without their bump and dagger-like *knitting sticks*, an old verse stating : "She knaws how to sing and knit/And she knaws how to carry t'kit/While she drives her kye to pasture." The industry declined during the 19th century.

L

Lady's Slipper : Rarest, most romantic of the Dales flora, the lady's slipper orchid (*Cypripꞏdium*) has for years hovered on the verge of extinction, mainly because of ruthless collection in its few really favoured places. This orchid bears seed which germinate after about nine years, and they take a further 16 years to flower.

Langstrothdale : The name is derived from a description, signifying a "long stretch of ground, marshy and overgrown with brushwood". Also known as Deepdale, this valley contains the nursery reaches of the river Wharfe, which forms with a merger of two becks at Beckermonds. The dale was inhabited by people of the Bronze and Iron Ages, who left traces behind them. A stone circle near Yockenthwaite is of Bronze Age origin. During Norman times the area, as "foresta de Langestrode", was a chase for wild beasts. Considerable planting with conifers is taking place beyond Beckermonds.

Lathe : From the Norse *hlatha,* a type of stone barn best seen in Swaledale.

Lead, Leadmining : (See MINING).

Limekilns : A fairly common feature of the limestone areas, where, during the 18th century particularly, but on into the 19th century, considerable quantities of lime were burnt using coal or coke as fuel. Lime and fuel were deposited within the tower in alternate layers. When fired, the material was left to burn itself out, being then extracted from the tunnel mouth. Lime was used as mortar for buildings and, spread on the land, sweetened the soil. Lime-burning this century has been undertaken at large, now well mechanised quarries, two large examples of which can be seen at Horton-in-Ribblesdale and at Swinden, near Threshfield.

Limestone Country : The largest outcrop of limestone in Britain occurs in the south and south-west parts of the National Park. Great Scar Limestone, of great purity, is the lowest deposition of the carboniferous group of rocks. Limestone scenery has impressive dry valleys, cliffs and scars, extensive pavements, potholes and caves. Growing at the base of outcrops and on screes is blue moorgrass; elsewhere, the sward in limestone counties is sweet and springy, changing little in its light green hue throughout the year. Ceaseless grazing by sheep tends to form a tight mass of vegetation. (See FAULTS, GEOLOGY).

Ling Gill : Small, well-wooded ravine cut into limestone at the head of Ribblesdale, and now a National Nature Reserve administered by the Nature Conservancy. The Gill is notable for its rich plant life. Trees include some mountain ash and bird cherry. (See COLT PARK).

Littondale : Tributary valley of the Wharfe, drained by the river Skirfare, which enters the river Wharfe at Amerdale Dub. William Wordsworth called the area Amerdale. To Charles Kingsley, writing in his book *The Water-Babies,* it was Vendale. The valley is named after a principal village.

Lynchets : The thousand-year-old cultivation terraces of the Anglian common fields. Ploughing could by itself produce such terracing. It is possible, however, that some construction work by the farmers was also necessary.

35

M

Malham Cove : Limestone cliffs 240 feet high, forming a headpiece for Malhamdale. The cove is a product of the mid-Craven fault. The stream which now emerges from its base originally went over the top and formed a waterfall.

Malham Tarn : Lies north of the North Craven fault. The water stands in what is conspicuously a limestone countryside because the bed of Malham Tarn is formed of impervious Silurian slate. The extent of the water is 153 acres and the height above sea level 1,200 feet. The maximum depth of water is 14 feet. Malham Tarn House is leased from the National Trust by the Field Studies Council. The overflow of the Tarn goes underground at the Water Sinks and reappears at Aire Head, below Malham.

Mastiles Lane : Track across Malham and Kilnsey moors. Mainly used by monastic settlements, it was marked by crosses. The bases of some crosses survive to this day.

Middleham Castle : Was once known as the Windsor of the North (being the main residence of Warwick the Kingmaker). The castle ruins are cared for by the government.

Millstone Grit : Coarse sandstones deposited over carboniferous limestone in the delta of an ancient river. In the limestone areas to the west it lies atop many of the fells; further east it dominates the countryside. The strata was named "millstone grit" because of its coarse nature and its use as millstones.

Mining : Among the Dales minerals which have been abstracted by commercial interests are lead ore (*galena*), barytes and fluorspar. There have been two main mining fields (1) Swaledale and Wensleydale, and (2) Upper Wharfedale, including Greenhow, and Malham.

Mining, Employment : Lead-mining was a labour-intensive industry that involved women and boys as well as men. Even women put in a 10-hour day! The boys first shovelled and barrowed *bouse* and were then taken into partnership by the men who bargained with the mine-owners over the rate to be paid for any lead abstracted. Working conditions in the lead mines were generally poor, the mines being constricted, badly-ventilated, often very wet. Wet mines were preferable to some dry mines where there was a heavy incidence of *gruver's complaint,* a form of silicosis.

Mining, Lead : There is evidence, from pigs of lead recovered from two places just outside the National Park, that the Romans mined lead, almost certainly using slave labour. A keen demand for lead developed in the 12th and 13th centuries, with exports to the South Country and the Continent. It was needed for roofing and other purposes involving building schemes. Lead merchants flourished in Richmond in Plantagenet times There was a considerable expansion of lead-mining during the 17th and 18th centuries, with output reaching its peak in the 19th century and declining from about 1860. Then, with a tariff wall removed, the importation of much cheap foreign ore began. Old lead workings are known in the Dales as *t'owd man.*

Mining, Silver : Lead ores hold a small percentage of silver. This was extracted after smelting. Lead yielding a high silver content came from mines at Appletreewick, Kettlewell (where one mine was known as Silver Rake), and Bishopdale. Several million ounces of silver were abstracted from Dales lead in the great mining period of 18th and 19th centuries.

Monastic Life : (See ABBEYS, PRIORIES).

Moors : The principal moors are between 1,000 and 1,250 feet above sea level. Here heather grows freely, attended by bilberry, crowberry, cowberry and cranberry, all good food for grouse, the best-known moorland bird. Heather moor is actually a desecrated countryside. Grazing by sheep — and regular burning, or *swiddening,* to keep a supply of fresh shoots — led to a monoculture and prevented a natural regeneration of the once-extensive woodland. *Nardus,* or white mat-grass, takes over in some overgrazed areas. The commonest species of heather is ling (*Calluna vulgaris*).

Mosses : (See COTTON GRASS BOGS).

N, O

National Park : A National Park exists for the preservation and enhancement of the landscape and to provide for the enjoyment of those seeking their pleasure in the area, always with proper regard to other land uses. The "architect" of National Park legislation, John Dower, did much of his study and writing in Malhamdale. The Dales National Park is one of five Parks without a coastline. It was designated in 1954, and extends over 680 square miles. The Park boundary extends from north of Skipton, passing to the east of the A.65, and just avoiding Settle and Ingleton. It extends to the old Yorkshire boundary, which it follows to Tan Hill. The Park boundary in the east takes in Arkengarthdale, Swaledale (but not Richmond), Wensleydale (to a point west of Wensley), Coverdale and Wharfedale (to Bolton Abbey).

Norsemen : A Scandinavian people who, arriving in England via the North Lancashire coastline during the 10th century, spread inland and took up marginal or high land in which Anglian and Danish settlers (who had earlier migrated from the east) were not interested. The Norsemen were less gregarious than the Angles. Mainly occupied with sheep farming, they moved with their flocks to high ground in summer so that the home acres could be left to grow grass for hay, the winter fodder, and also to avoid the summer fly menace. The percentage of names with Scandinavian roots decreases from west to east. Norsemen gave us the names fell, beck, gill, mere, moss, heath, ling. (See SAETR).

Oystercatcher : A handsome pied bird, with an orange-red bill and flesh-pink legs. In recent decades, this species has spread from the sea to nesting sites on shingle beside Dales rivers and streams.

Bolton Castle, Wensleydale (A. E. F. Wright)

P

Packhorses : Before the transport revolution early in the 19th century, packhorses were generally used for moving goods from place to place. A packhorse train usually consisted of between 20 and 40 animals. The animals included Jaeger ponies (of German origin), and the chief human attendant was called *jagger*. The use of such ponies with panniers was known in Swaledale as *jagging*. Loads carried by packhorses included peat, coal and lead. Some routes taken by packhorses have now developed into metalled motor roads; others remain green and lovely. Crossing points at streams were frequently simple single-span bridges.

Park Rash : Steep stretch of road with S-bends, leading from Kettlewelldale into Coverdale. "Park" relates to an enclosure made by the Nevilles for hunting purposes. "Rash" indicates a steep hill. This was on the coaching route from London to Richmond via Skipton. It is usable by cars, but has been banned to motor coaches on safety grounds.

Peat : The growth of peat was periodically rapid on the uplands between c.7000 B.C. and 1000 A.D. In places it lies 30 feet deep. Peat is formed by plant debris which, because of oxygen starvation (a consequence of the extreme wetness of the terrain), did not decompose in the normal way. From the peat comes evidence of old-time vegetation, notably birch. On some fell tops, the disturbance of peat such as by cutting and overgrazing has led to substantial wind-erosion. The right to take peat as fuel is known as *turbary*.

40

Penhill: A Wensleydale fell, its name of Celtic origin. On Penhill was one of Yorkshire's principal beacons, being associated with Roseberry Topping in Cleveland.

Pennines: Though popularly called a "chain" and "backbone of England," the Pennines represent a *broad uplift*, extending from Tyne to Trent, a distance of rather more than 120 miles. Many of the Southern peaks are over 1,000 feet above sea level. To the north of the Aire Gap (where converging valleys have broken the even run of hills at about the half way point) some fells stand at over 2,000 feet above sea level. The highest — Cross Fell, in Cumbria — is 2,930 feet. The name Pennine is derived from *Alpes Penina,* which appeared on a map alleged to be of Roman Britain. It was found to be an 18th century forgery.

Pennine Way: Britain's longest continuous footpath, extending for 250 miles from Edale (Derbyshire) to Stareough Hill above Kirk Yetholm (Roxburghshire). The idea of a Pennine Way was put forward in 1935 by Tom Stephenson; the route was surveyed in 1939, approved in 1951 but only completed in 1965. The National Parks Commission described the Pennine Way as "a strenuous high-level route through predominantly wild country and intended for walkers of some experience."

Penyghent: A lion-like fell dominating North Ribblesdale, being particularly well seen from Horton. Summit cairn at 2,273 feet. The name is derived from the Welsh, "pen" meaning a hill. Penyghent is the only fell of the famous Three Peaks group which is traversed by the Pennine Way. (See THREE PEAKS).

Placenames: Placenames were at first descriptive terms. They quickly became proper names. Among the oldest are Celtic terms, followed by those of the Angles and (from late in the 9th century) of the Norsemen. The Norman element assumed little importance. Later names derived from ecclesiastic Latin. Some placename elements associated with Dales features and settlements: Old Norse — *by* (farmstead, village), *griss* (young pig, as in Grisedale), *kelda* (spring, well), *mor* (moor), *sker* (scar), *topt* (enclosure), *thwait* (clearing). Old English — *ham* (homestead), *leah* (clearing in a wood), *stan* (stone), *stede* (site of a building, farm), *tun* (enclosure), farm, village, *wic* (dwelling, building, dairy farm).

Potholes: (See CAVES AND POTHOLES, GAPING GILL).

Priories: The best-known Priory, Bolton in Wharfedale, is incorrectly referred to today as an Abbey. The Priory of St. Mary at Bolton was occupied by canons of the Augustinian order, first founded at Embsay in 1120, then at Bolton in 1155; it was surrendered to the Crown in 1539. Two Swaledale priories were: Marrick, near Reeth (Benedictine nuns, 1154-1540) and Ellerton, on the opposite bank of the river (Cistercian nuns, who surrendered the priory to the Crown in 1536).

R - Z

Railways: During the "railway mania" of the 1840s, a line was laid from Darlington to Richmond (1846) and another up the Aire Valley to Skipton (1847). Leyburn in Wensleydale, was linked to Northallerton in 1856. Twenty years later, the railway had been extended to Hawes. The Settle-Carlisle railway was opened to passenger traffic in 1876, with a branch line to Hawes. The most impressive railway works in the Dales National Park are on the Settle-Carlisle railway, including Ribblehead viaduct (165 feet high), Blea Moor Tunnel (2,629 yards) and Dent station (1,145 feet above sea level). A branch railway line from Skipton to Grassington was opened in 1901 and was closed to passengers (apart from excursion trains) in 1930. Embsay railway station, near Skipton, has been preserved by the Dales Railway Company, Ltd.

Ring Ouzel: One of the summer hill birds, superficially resembling the blackbird but having a bold light crescent on its chest. The Pennine ring ouzels winter in North Africa; they return to the Dales in March.

Romans: There are comparatively few traces of Roman occupation in the Dales area. An important fort stood on Brough Hill, Bainbridge (Wensleydale). From here a road extended towards Lancaster over Cam End. The fort was established in 80 A.D. and used, with a short break, until the end of the occupation. It accommodated 500 infantry. There were Aire Gap forts at Ilkley and Elslack. A "marching camp" has been discovered by Mastiles Lane. Archaeologists have excavated extensively at Kirk Sink, Gargrave, where a Roman villa was established.

Saetr: The shieling or place where Norse people summered their stock. Three Wensleydale settlements with names derived from this practice are Appersett, Burtersett and Countersett. (See NORSEMEN).

Salmon: Attempts have been made to reintroduce salmon to the upper reaches of some Dales rivers from which the species was absent for many years. The farthest point reached inland from the East Coast is the headwaters of Bishopdale Beck, a tributary of the Ure. Salmon from the west coast can (with the help of "ladders" at Settle and near Langcliffe) spawn in the gravel beds of the Ribble around Selside, in North Ribblesdale. Salmon also run up the Lune, Rawthey, Dee and Clough.

Semerwater: Lake in a glaciated limestone valley near Bainbridge (Wensleydale). Maximum depth 34 feet, but generally 4 to 8 feet. Once there were lake dwellings here. Some disaster befalling them may have been responsible for a persistent legend of a drowned city, a story immortalised in verse by Sir William Watson (*Ballad of Semerwater*). A huge piece of limestone standing near the outflow of Semerwater is called the Carlow Stone; its present positioning was a consequence of glacial movement.

Sheep: For centuries the farmers of the upper dales have been pre-occupied by sheep — self-contained flocks of horned hill sheep that spend most of their year on the open fells. The ground is generally poor (1 sheep to several acres), but for a long period sheep represented virtually the only "crop" capable of showing a profit. Many former sheep grazings are now, however, planted with conifers, which are said to be more profitable. In the lower parts of the Dales, half-bred sheep are the rule.

Sheep Breeds: Foundation stock of the long-woolled hill sheep was the Scotch Blackface. Selective local breeding produced the several varieties. The *Swaledale* type, which shows a grey nose on a dark face, evolved on the old Yorkshire-Westmorland border, in the vicinity of Tan Hill. The Breeders' Association is now the largest of its kind in England. Slightly larger is the *Dalesbred,* the dark face of which has a splash of white on either side of the nostrils. This breed is commonly found in Craven. The thick-set *Rough Fell* is established mainly on the drier, harder fells about Sedbergh. Around but more particularly below the Aire Gap a visitor might see the *Lonk,* which is clearly a larger version of the Scotch Blackface.

Sheep Counting: Once believed to be Celtic in origin, the sheep-counting numerals may be post-medieval. *From Wharfedale* — yan, tan, tether, pathas, pimp, setha, letha, hova, dova, dik; yan-a-dik, tan-a-dik, tethra-dik, bomfit; yan-a-bomfit, tan-a-bomfit, teth-a-bomfit, path-a-bomfit, gigit. *From Rathmell, Ribblesdale* — aen, taen, tethra, fethera, phubs, aayther, layather, quoather, quaather, dugs;

44

aena-dugs, taena-dugs, tethra-dugs, fethera-dugs, buon; aena-buon, taena-buon, tethera-buon, fethera-buon, guu-a-guu. *From Middleton-in-Teesdale* — yan, tean, tether, mether, pip; lazar, azar, catrah, borna, dick; yan-a-dick, tean-a-dick, tethera-dick, methera-dick, dumfit; yan-a-bum, tean-a-dum, tethera-bum, methera-bum, jiggit.

Sheepdogs: Usually black and white, of the collie strain, and reputedly introduced to the Dales by Scotsmen engaged in droving. The working life of a sheepdog begins when it is between six months and two years old (some dogs are quicker on the uptake than others!). Four main commands must be learnt — right-hand turn, left-hand turn, stop and "come on." If conditions are good, a dog hears the whistle from a range of one and a half miles. A working dog might cover about 50 miles a day on the fells at gathering time. When several dogs are being worked at the same time, each responds to its private whistle code.

Sheep Nomenclature: A sheep is a lamb until it has been spained, or separated from its mother, when it becomes a hogg — gimmer hogg (female), wether hogg (castrated male) or tup hogg (male kept for breeding purposes). After the first clipping, the sheep is a shearling — gimmer shearling or shearling ram. The animal then acquires its first two broad teeth, or permanent incisors. After the next clipping, it is two shears, with four broad teeth. At three shears there are six broad teeth. At four shears an animal has eight teeth, or "full mouth."

Shepherds' Guides: Published for various areas of hill country, containing details of flock identification. Each flockmaster has his own personal marks: ear (lug) mark, horn burn, mark on the wool, sometimes all three. In some northern areas a sheep carries a mark to denote the *heaf* (or heugh) on which it lives.

Shepherds' Sticks : Also known as crooks. Handle is usually of tup's horn, picked up on the fells or removed from animals which have found them troublesome because of deformity. Boiling the horns softens it sufficiently for it to be shaped into the traditional crook pattern. Then it is sometimes carved. A lamb crook is between five and six feet long — much longer than the normal crook. The shaft is usually of hazel gathered at the "back-end" of the year.

Stainmore : The "stony moorland" between Edenvale and Teesdale. The course of the road follows a glacial cut groove, through which pieces of Shap granite were carried far to the east by glacial action. The route was used by men of the Bronze Age. To the Romans it was part of the road between York and Carlisle, with forts at Greta Bridge, Bowes and Brough.

Strid : A name said to derive from *stryth,* meaning a tumultuous rush of water. Here, between Barden and Bolton, the Wharfe is hemmed in by gritstone rocks for nearly a quarter of a mile. The river is only a few feet wide but 30 or more feet deep. Only foolhardy visitors jump across. There have been many fatalities.

Swale, river : Rises about half a mile from the springs of Eden and Ure, and in its 83 mile long course eastwards drains 576 square miles of country.

Tan Hill : Best-known because of its inn, the highest situated in England (1,732 feet above sea level). Historically, the hill has a long story, much of which is concerned with the exploitation of coal mines; hence there is a large number of converging roads. Coal was mined as early as the 13th century. The last of the local collieries closed down about 1932.

Trollers Gill : Limestone gorge near Parcevall Hall, Appletreewick, which (in Dales folklore) was the lair of the barguest, a spectral hound.   There is no right of way through this gorge.

Ure, river : Rises a mile or so from Hell Gill, near the source of the Eden, but unlike the Eden takes an easterly course through Wensleydale.   The river is $68\frac{1}{2}$ miles long, and its name was anciently rendered Yore.

Viewpoints : It has been claimed that both seas can be seen from some parts of the Dales. Buckden Pike offers a direct view of Humphrey Head, by Morecambe Bay, which is 36 miles away, and an eastward view of Teesmouth. An early 19th century guide-book claimed that both seas could be seen from the "towering eminence" of Water Crag, between Keld and Tan Hill.   Harry Speight, Victorian topographer, noted that from Tan Hill at night the coke ovens about Bishop Auckland might be clearly seen.

Walden : In a tributary valley of Wensleydale, being one of the remotest settlements.   It lies nearly six miles from West Burton.

Walls : A Dales drystone wall is really two walls in one. Each section stands side by side, being broader, more substantial at the base, where the *footings* are laid.   They are held together by large stones called *throughs,* which go from side to side of the wall. The wall is packed with *fillings* and surmounted by *topstones* or *capstones.* The hole left in some walls to allow for the passage of sheep is known in the West Riding as a *cripple-hole.*   Wall-building goes back to the earliest times.   There were monastic enclosures.   Crofts were made in connection with the Scottish droving trade. The refinement of the art of walling came during the enclosures of the common fields (mainly from 1780 to 1820).

Weather : Annual average rainfall of some Dales places, in inches : Ribblehead, 68; Malham Tarn, 58; Litton, 63;

Settle, 43.9; Burnsall, 41; Bolton Abbey, 36.3; Skipton, 32.9; Richmond, 28. Dr. G. S. Sweeting, who kept weather records in Littondale, reported that, on average, snow fell on 23 days each year, the main season being from January to March. The highest temperature he recorded in Littondale in any one year was 82 deg.f., on July 4, 1959.

West Stonesdale : Valley extending from Keld, in Swaledale, towards Tan Hill.

Wharfe, river : Source at springs on Cam Fell and Cush Knott, over 1,600 feet above sea level. It is not normally called Wharfe until the combining of the Greenfield and Oughtershaw becks at Beckermonds. The river drains 394 square miles of country.

Whaw : Curiously-named hamlet in Arkengarthdale. It is an Old Norse name indicating the enclosure near a fold.

Whernside : The highest peak in the Dales National Park, with a summit 2,414 feet above sea level. The name is derived from Old English, *cweorn,* meaning quern, relating to its millstone grit, which was once quarried for millstones.

Yoredale Series : Name given to the bands of limestone shales and sandstone which lie above the Great Scar Limestone. The name Yoredale Series was used by Phillips (1836), who studied them in Wensleydale, where they are particularly prominent. Here they give a conspicuously stepped appearance to fellsides.

Youth Hostels : The Association was founded in 1930 and has a string of hostels throughout the Dales. A hostel specially worthy of mention because of its grand situation is Garsdale Head, 1,250 feet above sea level near Hell Gill. The buildings lie over a mile from a metalled road.

Zinc : A mineral for which prospecting has taken place in the Dales in recent years.